MW00354658

RECORDS
TO THE *Rescue!*

A specific guide to the life of:

So that you can be more in control, someone can
assist you when you need help, and you can
have the confidence of knowing you are one step
ahead of whatever your future may hold.

CHRISTINE BALLARD

DEDICATION

In loving memory of my mother, Elizabeth "Betty" Ballard, who spent her short life caring for others. She died aged only 49 and left behind a host of men and women who still refer to her as their best friend, many years later.

This organizer is dedicated to all those who use it with her spirit and, either directly or indirectly, make someone's life easier or better as a result.

Copyright © 2015 by Christine H. Ballard
All rights reserved.
ISBN 978-0-9892366-3-8

Revised Edition

Published by The Orderly Office LLC
Printed in the USA

Book development and editing—Anne M. Carley of Chenille Books
Cover and book design—Gisela and Mark Swift of Picante Creative

This organizer is designed to guide the reader through the process of recording his or her own essential information. It is intended to be a useful record and ease the administrative burdens on family members, but it does not replace the need for proper legal documents. It is sold on the understanding that the author is not rendering legal or other professional advice—where this is required, the assistance of a qualified professional must always be sought.

ACKNOWLEDGMENTS

I am indebted to a great many people who have inspired, advised, guided, assisted, or encouraged me in the creation of this organizer.

At the head of the list must be my late father, Fred Ballard, whose sad situation made me so aware of the need for such a resource. Another guiding light has been my client and friend, Carla Sykes, whose fortitude and perseverance have never failed to inspire me.

I could not have created this organizer without the input of a team of professionals based in Charlottesville, VA, who had the necessary expertise to guide me through the multitude of small details required to make this a clear and effective tool. These include Beverley Butler, certified financial advisor and licensed social worker; Anne M. Carley of Chenille Books; Judy Grissmer, marriage and family therapist (retired) and licensed professional counselor (retired); Martha Haertig, EA; Elaine Kraus of Whole-Life Organizing; Dr. Andrew Macfarlan of Albemarle Square Family Health Care; Barry Slayton of The Apple Doctor; Eric D. Smith, attorney at law; Mary Stack, nurse practitioner; Mark and Gisela Swift of Picante Creative, and last but definitely not least, Bradford M. Young, attorney at law. My thanks go to each of you for advising, correcting, encouraging, and generally pointing me in the right direction!

I am also indebted to many other friends and clients whose contagious enthusiasm for the project prevented me from becoming discouraged.

And finally, a special thank-you to Michael V. E. Dunn for providing insight, suggestions, and encouragement, and for the many hours spent reviewing and improving the layout and text.

I offer my sincere thanks to each and every one of you.

Christine Ballard

{ C O N T E N T S }

The Basics

Estate Planning

Your Records

What's Next?

Notes

{THE BASICS}

Introduction

There are times in all of our lives when the comfortable, well-trodden carpet beneath our feet is pulled away, leaving us tumbling through the turmoil of a stressful and sometimes frightening new situation. This can happen at any age; we all know people whose lives have been shattered by divorce or death, illness, house fires, storms, hurricanes, tornados, floods, earthquakes, accidents or simply the effects of aging.

Most of us know that if we became incapacitated for any reason, our loved ones would not know where to begin to manage our affairs, and would have a daunting task on their hands.

In spite of this, we are usually only told to "get our affairs in order" when we are seriously ill or elderly. So, right when we are most vulnerable and confused, and when our time is most precious to us, we are expected to undertake this important task … and even then, no one tells us how to do it, or even where to start!

The intention of this organizer is to lead you through the process of obtaining and recording your important details and documents, noting where they are kept, and making it a specific guide to your life. It will enable you to be better in control; your loved ones will be able to use the organizer to help you when necessary, and you will have the confidence of knowing that you are one step ahead of any situation your future may hold.

Hopefully there will be a snowball effect, with everyone first completing their own organizer, and then giving the gift of time and love to friends and family who may need a little help in completing theirs.

Using this organizer

- Keep in mind that an incomplete organizer is better than no organizer at all, and that every single entry you make is a useful step forward.

- Because your information will change over time, I recommend using a pencil and eraser, or a pen and liquid paper, so that you can easily make alterations when necessary.

- You may choose to be methodical and work through the book from front to back, or you may choose to flip back and forth through the pages as you discover new information to add. Use the organizer as you wish and adapt it to make it yours. There is no right or wrong way of doing this.

- If you are married or have a partner, you may each want to have an organizer so that you can include your own personal information.

- If a section does not apply to you, leave it blank or adapt it for your own use.

- If you feel overwhelmed or are struggling to understand what to do, ask a trusted relative or friend to help you.

- Remember that this organizer will only help you in an emergency if one or two trusted family members or friends know that you have it and where to find it. List these names with their contact info in your mobile phone, your wallet, or vehicle's glove compartment as your ICE (in case of emergency) contacts.

- The information in this organizer should not be accessible to the wrong people. I therefore recommend you do not include sensitive information such as Social Security number, Employer ID number, bank account numbers, credit and debit card numbers or PIN numbers, and keep this organizer in a safe place where it can be found only by you and those you trust.

- Be aware that this organizer does not replace the need to consult a professional when necessary.

Choosing your team

Many of us manage our own affairs, choosing not to pay a third party to do something we can handle ourselves. There is nothing wrong with this choice … until a crisis occurs and these matters are left unattended.

But there is another option: gather a well-qualified team of professionals who can work with you. You can give them permission to communicate with each other, when necessary, so they can ensure your affairs are properly taken care of—even when you are ill, incapacitated, or just don't have the time or desire to deal with it yourself.

Here are five team members who could make your life easier:

The Attorney

It is possible to buy the paperwork needed to draw up your estate planning documents, fill in the blanks and have them notarized. If you do this, keep in mind that trying to do a will by yourself, without the help of an attorney, can leave your heirs arguing over exactly what was meant by your wording, and it increases the chance of litigation. Despite costing more, an attorney can make sure your documents are drawn up properly, with the correct wording to ensure they are valid, and will also offer advice that is specific to your situation. The attorney can discuss which documents you need, explain how best to take advantage of laws and regulations that will affect your estate when you die, and make sure your wishes are represented accurately in the wording.

The Financial Advisor

Although some of us are perfectly competent to manage our own finances, if we want to simplify our lives and reduce stress, we can consider paying a financial advisor to work with us and help us achieve our financial goals. It is important to understand that anyone can call themselves a financial advisor, so you should always choose a person who is registered as a Certified Financial Advisor and has the skills and experience necessary to help you with your particular needs.

Some financial advisors do not manage your money, so you retain the responsibility of seeking their advice when you feel it necessary, acting on their advice only if you choose to do so. These advisors usually charge by the hour. On the other hand, advisors providing full management of your investments generally charge a commission on trading activity and/or a percentage of your total portfolio value.

It is therefore important to first have a clear understanding of what help you need, and then seek recommendations from friends or other professionals. Interview those recommended candidates until you are confident you have the right one for you.

The Tax Preparer

While some people successfully file their own taxes, an easier and less stressful option is to file with the help of the same tax preparer each year. The advantage of doing so is that the tax preparer will get to know your particular circumstances and therefore be better able to offer advice, support, and guidance. Also, if you are ever audited, the preparer will be able to help you through the process, and if you

choose a preparer with EA or CPA credentials, he or she can represent you before the Internal Revenue Service. Finally, should anything happen to you, your tax preparer will be able to assist your spouse, power of attorney, or executor to ensure your tax issues are managed properly.

The Primary Care Physician

Over the years, we seem to collect doctors and specialists for different ailments, so ideally we need a primary care physician who knows us well and takes on the role of "conductor of the orchestra." In a medical crisis, it would be best to have one doctor who can give full information and act as your medical ally.

Other Services

You may be able to find other local organizations or businesses that offer services to make your life easier. They may offer help with daily money management, home or office organizing, child care, personal care, companion care, transportation to and from appointments, shopping, obtaining prescription medications, and much more. It is worth knowing what is available in your area.

{ ESTATE **PLANNING** }

Estate planning documents

*T*here are four estate planning documents essential to ensure that your wishes are followed if you are unable to manage your own affairs, or if you die. See page 118 to record your own information.

- **A will and/or trust,** which explains what should happen to your estate when you die.

- **Durable general power of attorney,** which gives someone of your choosing permission to take over the management of your affairs. If you make it effective immediately, you must really trust the person you name. Another way is to make it effective only if you become incapacitated, in which case the person named must get a doctor's note every six months to prove that you are still incapacitated.

- **Medical power of attorney,** which gives someone of your choosing permission to make medical decisions for you if you are unable to do so yourself.

- **Advance medical directive** (sometimes called a "living will"), which tells everyone how you want to be medically treated if you reach the point where you are unaware of yourself or your surroundings and have no hope of recovery, or if you are dying and unable to communicate end-of-life decisions.

In addition to these four documents, it is recommended that you also leave the following information:

- **Details of your prepaid funeral plan, or a note of your funeral wishes** stating your preference regarding burial or cremation, and what kind of ceremony you want. This removes unnecessary stress from your loved ones at a time when stress is already high.

- **A list of special items** (specifically referenced in your will or trust) that you would like to leave to particular people. This may include jewelry, antiques, or simply something of sentimental value, with no great monetary worth at all.

Estate planning tips

- Keep in mind that rules differ from state to state. It is always best to consult an attorney to ensure that you have the right documents with the right wording for your personal situation in your particular state. Doing this ensures that what you want to happen on your death really will happen ... and that it does so without leaving headaches and conflict between your heirs. Trying to make your will by yourself, without the help of an attorney, can leave heirs arguing over what was meant by your will—this is especially true if you have a home and other assets of value.

- A properly drawn-up will should include your advance medical directive; medical power of attorney; durable general power of attorney; instructions regarding organ donation; and a list of important personal possessions, noting to whom they are left. However, if you only want to arrange medical power of attorney and your advance medical directive, you can ask your family doctor or hospital to help you complete the necessary forms—you do not need an attorney to do this.

- If you have retirement or other accounts, you may want to name primary and secondary beneficiaries when possible. This may allow the funds to be transferred directly to the beneficiary upon your death, rather than going through probate (the court system) as part of your estate—which is often a long process.

- Someone will have to pay the cost of transporting larger items such as furniture, if they have been left to heirs. You can state in your will whether you want the heir receiving each piece to pay these costs, or if you want the costs to be taken from the estate.

- When deciding how to distribute your assets, be they investment accounts, retirement accounts, real estate or your personal property, it is worth finding out how each will be taxed, or if special inheritance rules apply. This will affect how much your beneficiaries receive—an important consideration if you want to leave equal amounts to different beneficiaries.

- In order to reduce the possibility of any conflict amongst your heirs, you can leave a list of important personal possessions specifying which person should inherit each item. In order to be legally binding, this list must be properly signed and dated, and be specifically incorporated into your will. It is best to use an attorney who can ensure that the list is prepared properly. As time goes on and your situation changes, you should update your list and destroy the old one to avoid any confusion.

- If you want to ensure that the surviving spouse or partner will be able to stay in your home after one of you dies, ask your attorney to make sure you have the right documents with the right wording to ensure that this will happen. It may not be enough simply to have the home in both names.

- If you believe that your heirs will argue or fight over the will, your attorney can help you include a 'no-contest' clause. This means that anyone who contests your will forfeits his or her inheritance. You can either warn them so they won't contest it, or let them find out the hard way!

- It is essential that all people with minor children or other dependents name a surrogate guardian in their will in case both parents, or caregivers, die. Your attorney will advise you on how to provide for them.

- Sometimes estate planning documents are left with an attorney but are not referred to upon death because no one else knows they exist. Be sure to complete the document locator chart in this organizer to prevent this, and also tell your loved ones where your documents can be found.

- People with pets often name a surrogate guardian for them in their will. If you do this, you may want to leave money to the person named to cover the costs of pet care.

- If there is estate tax to be paid, you can state in your will that such tax is to be paid from the estate, so that your heirs won't be responsible for paying for it themselves.

- Do not mark, write on, or staple anything to your original will or trust documents, because this may render them invalid.

- Revisit your estate planning documents every five years or so, to add updates or make amendments.

- If you replace an old will with a new one, destroy the old one. This is important because, if your heirs find the old one first, they could assume it is correct and then fail to look for an updated version.

Where to keep estate planning documents

O nce you have gone to the trouble of having documents drawn up, you must make sure that they are kept in a safe place, and that the right people can find them when they are needed. Be sure to complete the document locator chart (page 134), which records where each of your documents is kept.

The following list describes five locations for you to consider. Depending upon the document, you may choose to keep the original in one place and keep copies elsewhere.

A secure place at home

You may choose to keep your documents in your home because it is more convenient for you. If you do this, I recommend using a locked, fireproof, and waterproof box. Keep in mind that if something happens to you, the documents (especially your medical power of attorney, advance medical directive, and funeral wishes) will be needed quickly, so it is best to let the right people know where this box and its key can be found.

A bank safe deposit box

Banks charge an annual fee for renting a bank safe deposit box, with the cost dependent upon the size of box you choose. You receive a box number and a key—you can either choose to be the only person allowed to open it, or you can name someone else you trust to have joint access, with their own key.

It is best to ask your particular bank what happens to your box if you die or become incapacitated, because rules may differ and may change over time. You may find that if you are the only person with access to your box, or if the other person with joint access is not available to open your box, your loved ones may have trouble retrieving important documents (such as your advance medical directive, durable general or medical power of attorney documents, funeral instructions, or your will). Consequently, it may be wise to give someone else joint access, and as an added precaution, to keep original documents that may need to be produced quickly in a more accessible place.

Your attorney's office

If your estate planning documents are kept at your attorney's office, it is very important that other people know where they are. If no one knows where they are, the attorney may never be contacted, and the documents may never be seen. If the attorney has the originals, it is a good idea to keep copies elsewhere stating where the originals are held.

However, it is worth bearing in mind that your attorney may retire or die. Should this happen, you will need to know who has taken over their duties, or if they are sole practitioners, what arrangements have been made for the retention of your records.

Your primary care physician's office and the local hospital

It is best to leave a copy of your advance medical directive with your primary care physician, and another in the medical records department of local and other hospitals you may use. This enables medical professionals to give you the kind of medical treatment you want, even if you are not able to communicate.

Online registry

Some states provide secure, confidential online registries allowing subscribers to input information about their advance health care directive, medical power of attorney, and organ donation wishes. This registry allows emergency responders, doctors, and family members of your choosing to obtain such details. You can either search the Internet or ask your attorney if such a service exists in your area.

Some original documents will need to be accessed quickly in the event of an emergency or your death. Therefore, you may want to consider keeping instructions such as your original durable general and medical power of attorney documents, your original living will, your organ donation and funeral wishes, and your obituary notes in a secure place at home, with copies elsewhere. It is very important that these originals can be found quickly when needed.

What happens if you don't have estate planning documents?

- If you don't have a will, the assets you own will be distributed according to the law of the particular state in which you live. This may not be how you expect (or want) them to be distributed. Your spouse or partner may even find that they are not able to remain in the family home. You will not have legally named guardians for minor children, or dependents, should both parents die. Additionally, you will not have been able to leave a legally binding list of your prized possessions, stating to whom you wish to leave them—which may lead to rivalry, or even lawsuits, amongst your heirs.

- If you don't have a durable general power of attorney document, and you become unable to manage your own finances and other assets, your family may have to petition the courts to obtain power of attorney. The courts will have to decide who should be appointed conservator and have the power to manage your affairs for you. This process takes time and can cost several thousand dollars, and the power may be given to someone you would not choose—so it is better for you to make this decision now and name the person you want, while you still can.

- If you don't have medical power of attorney documents, and you are unable to make

medical decisions for yourself, the law of the particular state in which you live may dictate who makes these decisions for you. In addition, someone may initiate court proceedings to be appointed guardian of your person and gain the authority to make your health care decisions. This may be someone you would not choose, so it is better to decide which person you trust to take on this responsibility and name them while you can.

- If you don't have an advance medical directive, your spouse and/or children may be put in the extremely difficult position of having to decide, and agree upon, what kind of end-of-life medical treatment you should have. This scenario can cause terrible family rifts and unnecessary stress and expense. You may also end up receiving treatments you would not choose.

- If you don't have funeral wishes in writing, the planning and decisions will be left to your family or friends. If they can't agree, this can cause extra stress and family rifts at a time when stress levels are already high. Furthermore, some states will not allow cremation if you have not left written instructions, even if your family members or friends know that you wished to be cremated.

{ Y O U R **R E C O R D S** }

Recording the details of your life

*T*he remainder of this organizer, which represents the main body of the work, is designed to be adapted for your own personal requirements.

The sections are intended to guide you through the task of recording each set of essential details. They begin with personal issues and then cover your family, home, possessions, finances, commitments, health issues, estate planning, and conclude with end-of-life plans and the location of documents. Each section begins with an example, followed by ample blank workbook space in which to insert your own data. There are pages at the end for extra notes.

Completing this organizer is best achieved over a gentle period of time rather than in one daunting session, but it's worth the effort—both for you and your loved ones. Remember that any information you include is better than no information at all. Do remember, though, to keep it all up to date!

PERSONAL

This section records how to contact your important people in the event of an emergency.

At least one person listed should have access to your house and know about this organizer, especially if you have children or pets, so they can make sure all is cared for as you would want it to be.

If you have a place of worship, you may wish to include the name and contact information of your minister or religious leader.

Adapt this section to your own personal situation and make it truly your own.

EXAMPLE

NAME	Jane Doe	NOTES
RELATIONSHIP	My daughter	I would want Jane to look after my household in an emergency.
CONTACT INFO	XXX-XXX-XXXX (mobile)	

NAME	Jill	NOTES
RELATIONSHIP	My friend	
CONTACT INFO	XXX-XXX-XXXX (mobile)	

NAME	Julie Smith	NOTES
RELATIONSHIP	My neighbor	Julie has a key to my house.
CONTACT INFO	XXX-XXX-XXXX (mobile)	

NAME	NOTES
RELATIONSHIP	
CONTACT INFO	

NAME	NOTES
RELATIONSHIP	
CONTACT INFO	

NAME	NOTES
RELATIONSHIP	
CONTACT INFO	

NAME	NOTES
RELATIONSHIP	
CONTACT INFO	

NAME	NOTES
RELATIONSHIP	
CONTACT INFO	

NAME		NOTES
RELATIONSHIP		
CONTACT INFO		

NAME		NOTES
RELATIONSHIP		
CONTACT INFO		

NAME		NOTES
RELATIONSHIP		
CONTACT INFO		

NAME		NOTES
RELATIONSHIP		
CONTACT INFO		

NAME		NOTES
RELATIONSHIP		
CONTACT INFO		

NAME	NOTES
RELATIONSHIP	
CONTACT INFO	

NAME	NOTES
RELATIONSHIP	
CONTACT INFO	

NAME	NOTES
RELATIONSHIP	
CONTACT INFO	

NAME	NOTES
RELATIONSHIP	
CONTACT INFO	

NAME	NOTES
RELATIONSHIP	
CONTACT INFO	

DEPENDENTS

In this section you should note the names of, and brief details about, children and adults who are dependent on your being there for them. This should include the contact information of someone who has agreed, temporarily or permanently, to care for them in an emergency situation.

It is essential that people with minor children name a guardian for them in their will, in case both parents die or are incapacitated. Similar arrangements should also be made for other dependents requiring a guardian. This must be worded correctly for the rules and regulations of your particular state, so consulting an attorney is essential. If what you write here is different from that written in your will, the will takes priority because it is legally binding, whereas this section is simply a non-legally binding statement of your wishes that may be helpful in a crisis. It is best to ensure that the information given here reflects the wording of your will.

If your dependent person has special needs, it may be more difficult to name a suitable surrogate guardian, and if you are in this position you need to have other plans in place. You will want to take into consideration his or her future physical, emotional, financial, and spiritual wellbeing. You can discuss your situation with family, friends, medical personnel, counselors, therapists, organizations, support groups, community services, financial advisors, attorneys, or spiritual leaders, to identify your options. As difficult as this is, you have to pick the best option available and prepare for it in every way possible. Emergency caregivers should understand the plan and know how to implement it. It would be helpful to complete a separate organizer for your dependent so all his or her information is recorded in one place, and then ensure that the emergency caregiver knows where to find it.

EXAMPLE

NAME/AGE	James Doe/25	NOTES
RELATIONSHIP	My son	James lives with me and has autism. Jenny knows where to find his organizer and knows what to do.
EMERGENCY CAREGIVER'S NAME AND PHONE NUMBER	Jenny Doe (my younger sister), XXX-XXX-XXXX (mobile)	

NAME/AGE	NOTES
RELATIONSHIP	
EMERGENCY CAREGIVER'S NAME AND PHONE NUMBER	

NAME/AGE	NOTES
RELATIONSHIP	
EMERGENCY CAREGIVER'S NAME AND PHONE NUMBER	

NAME/AGE	NOTES
RELATIONSHIP	
EMERGENCY CAREGIVER'S NAME AND PHONE NUMBER	

NAME/AGE	NOTES
RELATIONSHIP	
EMERGENCY CAREGIVER'S NAME AND PHONE NUMBER	

NAME/AGE		NOTES
RELATIONSHIP		
EMERGENCY CAREGIVER'S NAME AND PHONE NUMBER		

NAME/AGE		NOTES
RELATIONSHIP		
EMERGENCY CAREGIVER'S NAME AND PHONE NUMBER		

NAME/AGE		NOTES
RELATIONSHIP		
EMERGENCY CAREGIVER'S NAME AND PHONE NUMBER		

NAME/AGE		NOTES
RELATIONSHIP		
EMERGENCY CAREGIVER'S NAME AND PHONE NUMBER		

NAME/AGE

NOTES

RELATIONSHIP

EMERGENCY
CAREGIVER'S
NAME AND
PHONE NUMBER

NAME/AGE

NOTES

RELATIONSHIP

EMERGENCY
CAREGIVER'S
NAME AND
PHONE NUMBER

NAME/AGE

NOTES

RELATIONSHIP

EMERGENCY
CAREGIVER'S
NAME AND
PHONE NUMBER

NAME/AGE

NOTES

RELATIONSHIP

EMERGENCY
CAREGIVER'S
NAME AND
PHONE NUMBER

PETS AND LIVESTOCK

Anyone who loves their pets or cares for livestock will want to ensure that they are safe, and taken care of by the right people, in an emergency situation.

In this section you should list all pets and livestock, and their details, along with the name of the pet sitter or livestock help you use, and the contact information for their veterinarian. You may also want to include the name of a person willing to take care of them, either temporarily or permanently, if necessary.

If you are not able to name someone willing to care for your pets, you might note that you want them to go to a no-kill SPCA, who will find appropriate new homes for them.

Remember that details listed here are simply an indication of your intent and are not legally binding. Most people with pets or livestock leave instructions regarding their future care as part of their will, which *is* legally binding. They often leave money to those who agree to look after them, to cover the cost of care.

EXAMPLE

NAME, YEAR OF BIRTH, AND DESCRIPTION	Buddy (2013), Black and white male border collie dog	NOTES
EMERGENCY CAREGIVER'S NAME AND PHONE NUMBER	Jane Doe (my daughter) XXX-XXX-XXXX (mobile)	Vet is Dr. Petem, phone XXX-XXX-XXXX. Jane would take Buddy permanently if necessary.

NAME, YEAR OF BIRTH, AND DESCRIPTION	Mister (2012), male chestnut pony	NOTES
EMERGENCY CAREGIVER'S NAME AND PHONE NUMBER	Dawn Ryzer of Hoofit Boarding Stables XXX-XXX-XXXX (office) XXX-XXX-XXXX (mobile)	Mister is already boarded with Dawn. She arranges vet and would look for an appropriate home for him if necessary.

NAME, YEAR OF BIRTH, AND DESCRIPTION		NOTES
EMERGENCY CAREGIVER'S NAME AND PHONE NUMBER		

NAME, YEAR OF BIRTH, AND DESCRIPTION		NOTES
EMERGENCY CAREGIVER'S NAME AND PHONE NUMBER		

NAME, YEAR OF BIRTH, AND DESCRIPTION		NOTES
EMERGENCY CAREGIVER'S NAME AND PHONE NUMBER		

NAME, YEAR OF BIRTH, AND DESCRIPTION		NOTES
EMERGENCY CAREGIVER'S NAME AND PHONE NUMBER		

NAME, YEAR OF BIRTH, AND DESCRIPTION		NOTES
EMERGENCY CAREGIVER'S NAME AND PHONE NUMBER		

NAME, YEAR OF BIRTH, AND DESCRIPTION		NOTES
EMERGENCY CAREGIVER'S NAME AND PHONE NUMBER		

NAME, YEAR OF BIRTH, AND DESCRIPTION		NOTES
EMERGENCY CAREGIVER'S NAME AND PHONE NUMBER		

NAME, YEAR OF BIRTH, AND DESCRIPTION		NOTES
EMERGENCY CAREGIVER'S NAME AND PHONE NUMBER		

NAME, YEAR OF BIRTH, AND DESCRIPTION		NOTES
EMERGENCY CAREGIVER'S NAME AND PHONE NUMBER		

NAME, YEAR OF BIRTH, AND DESCRIPTION		NOTES
EMERGENCY CAREGIVER'S NAME AND PHONE NUMBER		

NAME, YEAR OF BIRTH, AND DESCRIPTION		NOTES
EMERGENCY CAREGIVER'S NAME AND PHONE NUMBER		

NAME, YEAR OF BIRTH, AND DESCRIPTION		NOTES
EMERGENCY CAREGIVER'S NAME AND PHONE NUMBER		

PRIMARY HOME

This section provides you with a concise summary of your business contacts and details relating to your primary home.

Everyone's situation is different, but you may well want to include such things as insurance, landline and mobile phone services, electricity, water and gas companies, heating maintenance agreements, lawn care service, gardener, cleaning service, home help, caregivers, trash removal, home security system, Internet service, computer antivirus service, TV service, movie rental agreements, home association dues, landlord's contact information, and anything else that you think is relevant for you and your primary home.

Loans and mortgages will be included in the Financial section of this organizer (page 54).

EXAMPLE

SERVICE	water	NOTES
COMPANY AND CONTACT INFO	Trickelon Water Authority Tel: XXX-XXX-XXXX	www.trickleonwater.com
ACCOUNT #	XXXXXXXXXXX	
PAYMENT METHOD	automatic payment from checking account	
PAYMENT DUE DATE	monthly on 12th	

SERVICE	NOTES
COMPANY AND CONTACT INFO	
ACCOUNT #	
PAYMENT METHOD	
PAYMENT DUE DATE	

SERVICE	NOTES
COMPANY AND CONTACT INFO	
ACCOUNT #	
PAYMENT METHOD	
PAYMENT DUE DATE	

SERVICE	NOTES
COMPANY AND CONTACT INFO	
ACCOUNT #	
PAYMENT METHOD	
PAYMENT DUE DATE	

SERVICE		NOTES
COMPANY AND CONTACT INFO		
ACCOUNT #		
PAYMENT METHOD		
PAYMENT DUE DATE		

SERVICE		NOTES
COMPANY AND CONTACT INFO		
ACCOUNT #		
PAYMENT METHOD		
PAYMENT DUE DATE		

SERVICE		NOTES
COMPANY AND CONTACT INFO		
ACCOUNT #		
PAYMENT METHOD		
PAYMENT DUE DATE		

SERVICE

NOTES

COMPANY AND
CONTACT INFO

ACCOUNT #

PAYMENT METHOD

PAYMENT DUE DATE

SERVICE

NOTES

COMPANY AND
CONTACT INFO

ACCOUNT #

PAYMENT METHOD

PAYMENT DUE DATE

SERVICE

NOTES

COMPANY AND
CONTACT INFO

ACCOUNT #

PAYMENT METHOD

PAYMENT DUE DATE

SERVICE		NOTES
COMPANY AND CONTACT INFO		
ACCOUNT #		
PAYMENT METHOD		
PAYMENT DUE DATE		

SERVICE		NOTES
COMPANY AND CONTACT INFO		
ACCOUNT #		
PAYMENT METHOD		
PAYMENT DUE DATE		

SERVICE		NOTES
COMPANY AND CONTACT INFO		
ACCOUNT #		
PAYMENT METHOD		
PAYMENT DUE DATE		

SERVICE	NOTES
COMPANY AND CONTACT INFO	
ACCOUNT #	
PAYMENT METHOD	
PAYMENT DUE DATE	

SERVICE	NOTES
COMPANY AND CONTACT INFO	
ACCOUNT #	
PAYMENT METHOD	
PAYMENT DUE DATE	

SERVICE	NOTES
COMPANY AND CONTACT INFO	
ACCOUNT #	
PAYMENT METHOD	
PAYMENT DUE DATE	

SERVICE		NOTES
COMPANY AND CONTACT INFO		
ACCOUNT #		
PAYMENT METHOD		
PAYMENT DUE DATE		

SERVICE		NOTES
COMPANY AND CONTACT INFO		
ACCOUNT #		
PAYMENT METHOD		
PAYMENT DUE DATE		

SERVICE		NOTES
COMPANY AND CONTACT INFO		
ACCOUNT #		
PAYMENT METHOD		
PAYMENT DUE DATE		

SERVICE	NOTES
COMPANY AND CONTACT INFO	
ACCOUNT #	
PAYMENT METHOD	
PAYMENT DUE DATE	

SERVICE	NOTES
COMPANY AND CONTACT INFO	
ACCOUNT #	
PAYMENT METHOD	
PAYMENT DUE DATE	

SERVICE	NOTES
COMPANY AND CONTACT INFO	
ACCOUNT #	
PAYMENT METHOD	
PAYMENT DUE DATE	

SECONDARY HOMES

This section is similar to the one for the primary home but gives details and contacts for anything connected with your second home, if you have one.

You may want to include details about a property manager, the cleaning service, insurance, phone services, electricity, water and gas companies, heating maintenance company, lawn care service, gardener, trash removal, home security system, Internet service, computer antivirus service, TV service, movie rental service, home association dues, etc. If the home is privately rented out, you could list the details of the current renters.

Again, everyone's situation will be different, so you should adapt the details to fit your own personal situation. As some people have more than one secondary home, there is a space at the top of each page in which to note the address.

Information about mortgages should be included in the Financial section of this workbook (page 54).

EXAMPLE

ADDRESS: 2223 Leaping Deer Drive, Dunton, VA 22987 ....

SERVICE	Property Manager	NOTES
COMPANY AND CONTACT INFO	C. Tewit's Property Management Co, Tel: XXX-XXX-XXXX	They manage renters, income, repairs, complaints, cleaning and upkeep.
ACCOUNT #		
PAYMENT METHOD	Deducted from rental income	
PAYMENT DUE DATE		

ADDRESS: ....

SERVICE	NOTES
COMPANY AND CONTACT INFO	
ACCOUNT #	
PAYMENT METHOD	
PAYMENT DUE DATE	

SERVICE	NOTES
COMPANY AND CONTACT INFO	
ACCOUNT #	
PAYMENT METHOD	
PAYMENT DUE DATE	

SERVICE	NOTES
COMPANY AND CONTACT INFO	
ACCOUNT #	
PAYMENT METHOD	
PAYMENT DUE DATE	

ADDRESS: ....

SERVICE		NOTES
COMPANY AND CONTACT INFO		
ACCOUNT #		
PAYMENT METHOD		
PAYMENT DUE DATE		

SERVICE		NOTES
COMPANY AND CONTACT INFO		
ACCOUNT #		
PAYMENT METHOD		
PAYMENT DUE DATE		

SERVICE		NOTES
COMPANY AND CONTACT INFO		
ACCOUNT #		
PAYMENT METHOD		
PAYMENT DUE DATE		

ADDRESS: ....

SERVICE	NOTES
COMPANY AND CONTACT INFO	
ACCOUNT #	
PAYMENT METHOD	
PAYMENT DUE DATE	

SERVICE	NOTES
COMPANY AND CONTACT INFO	
ACCOUNT #	
PAYMENT METHOD	
PAYMENT DUE DATE	

SERVICE	NOTES
COMPANY AND CONTACT INFO	
ACCOUNT #	
PAYMENT METHOD	
PAYMENT DUE DATE	

ADDRESS: ....

SERVICE		NOTES
COMPANY AND CONTACT INFO		
ACCOUNT #		
PAYMENT METHOD		
PAYMENT DUE DATE		

SERVICE		NOTES
COMPANY AND CONTACT INFO		
ACCOUNT #		
PAYMENT METHOD		
PAYMENT DUE DATE		

SERVICE		NOTES
COMPANY AND CONTACT INFO		
ACCOUNT #		
PAYMENT METHOD		
PAYMENT DUE DATE		

ADDRESS: ....

SERVICE	NOTES
COMPANY AND CONTACT INFO	
ACCOUNT #	
PAYMENT METHOD	
PAYMENT DUE DATE	

SERVICE	NOTES
COMPANY AND CONTACT INFO	
ACCOUNT #	
PAYMENT METHOD	
PAYMENT DUE DATE	

SERVICE	NOTES
COMPANY AND CONTACT INFO	
ACCOUNT #	
PAYMENT METHOD	
PAYMENT DUE DATE	

ADDRESS: ....

SERVICE		NOTES
COMPANY AND CONTACT INFO		
ACCOUNT #		
PAYMENT METHOD		
PAYMENT DUE DATE		

SERVICE		NOTES
COMPANY AND CONTACT INFO		
ACCOUNT #		
PAYMENT METHOD		
PAYMENT DUE DATE		

SERVICE		NOTES
COMPANY AND CONTACT INFO		
ACCOUNT #		
PAYMENT METHOD		
PAYMENT DUE DATE		

ADDRESS: ....

SERVICE	NOTES
COMPANY AND CONTACT INFO	
ACCOUNT #	
PAYMENT METHOD	
PAYMENT DUE DATE	

SERVICE	NOTES
COMPANY AND CONTACT INFO	
ACCOUNT #	
PAYMENT METHOD	
PAYMENT DUE DATE	

SERVICE	NOTES
COMPANY AND CONTACT INFO	
ACCOUNT #	
PAYMENT METHOD	
PAYMENT DUE DATE	

VEHICLES

In this section you may record information about your vehicles, including cars, trucks, farm vehicles, mopeds or motorbikes, bicycles, recreational vehicles, boats and watercraft, and even airplanes. Use the space at the top of each page to note which vehicle the information on that page refers to.

Use the spaces to identify your insurer, car loan company, emergency service, dealership or mechanic for maintenance and repair, warranty details, and all other relevant services.

Details about any loans for purchasing vehicles could be included in the Financial section on page 54.

EXAMPLE

VEHICLE MAKE, COLOR, MODEL & YEAR: *Red, 2014, Wanna Convertible*

LICENSE # (REGISTRATION): XXX XXXX

VIN: XXXXXXXXXXXXXXX

WHERE GARAGED: *at my home*

SERVICE	Repairs and maintenance	NOTES
COMPANY AND PHONE NUMBER	C. Yougo's Repair Service Tel: XXX-XXX-XXXX	I keep a record of work done in the glove compartment.
ACCOUNT #	12987	
PAYMENT METHOD	Credit card	
PAYMENT DUE DATE	When invoiced	

VEHICLE MAKE, COLOR, MODEL & YEAR: ....

LICENSE # (REGISTRATION): ....

VIN: ....

WHERE GARAGED: ....

SERVICE	NOTES
COMPANY AND PHONE NUMBER	
ACCOUNT #	
PAYMENT METHOD	
PAYMENT DUE DATE	

SERVICE	NOTES
COMPANY AND PHONE NUMBER	
ACCOUNT #	
PAYMENT METHOD	
PAYMENT DUE DATE	

SERVICE	NOTES
COMPANY AND PHONE NUMBER	
ACCOUNT #	
PAYMENT METHOD	
PAYMENT DUE DATE	

VEHICLE MAKE, COLOR, MODEL & YEAR: ....

LICENSE # (REGISTRATION): ....

VIN: ....

WHERE GARAGED: ....

SERVICE		NOTES
COMPANY AND PHONE NUMBER		
ACCOUNT #		
PAYMENT METHOD		
PAYMENT DUE DATE		

SERVICE		NOTES
COMPANY AND PHONE NUMBER		
ACCOUNT #		
PAYMENT METHOD		
PAYMENT DUE DATE		

SERVICE		NOTES
COMPANY AND PHONE NUMBER		
ACCOUNT #		
PAYMENT METHOD		
PAYMENT DUE DATE		

VEHICLE MAKE, COLOR, MODEL & YEAR: ....

LICENSE # (REGISTRATION): ....

VIN: ....

WHERE GARAGED: ....

SERVICE	NOTES
COMPANY AND PHONE NUMBER	
ACCOUNT #	
PAYMENT METHOD	
PAYMENT DUE DATE	

SERVICE	NOTES
COMPANY AND PHONE NUMBER	
ACCOUNT #	
PAYMENT METHOD	
PAYMENT DUE DATE	

SERVICE	NOTES
COMPANY AND PHONE NUMBER	
ACCOUNT #	
PAYMENT METHOD	
PAYMENT DUE DATE	

VEHICLE MAKE, COLOR, MODEL & YEAR: ....

LICENSE # (REGISTRATION): ....

VIN: ....

WHERE GARAGED: ....

SERVICE		NOTES
COMPANY AND PHONE NUMBER		
ACCOUNT #		
PAYMENT METHOD		
PAYMENT DUE DATE		

SERVICE		NOTES
COMPANY AND PHONE NUMBER		
ACCOUNT #		
PAYMENT METHOD		
PAYMENT DUE DATE		

SERVICE		NOTES
COMPANY AND PHONE NUMBER		
ACCOUNT #		
PAYMENT METHOD		
PAYMENT DUE DATE		

VEHICLE MAKE, COLOR, MODEL & YEAR: ....

LICENSE # (REGISTRATION): ....

VIN: ....

WHERE GARAGED: ....

SERVICE	NOTES
COMPANY AND PHONE NUMBER	
ACCOUNT #	
PAYMENT METHOD	
PAYMENT DUE DATE	

SERVICE	NOTES
COMPANY AND PHONE NUMBER	
ACCOUNT #	
PAYMENT METHOD	
PAYMENT DUE DATE	

SERVICE	NOTES
COMPANY AND PHONE NUMBER	
ACCOUNT #	
PAYMENT METHOD	
PAYMENT DUE DATE	

IMPORTANT POSSESSIONS

When someone dies and his or her house is cleared, belongings that are not seen to be of value may be thrown away. However, if you own certain items that are financially valuable, of historical interest, or of sentimental value, you may record them in this section. Also, if you know the history of a special belonging, write it down in this section as well. Try to include how you acquired it, the name of the maker or artist, who owned it before you, its value, or why it is of sentimental value.

If you want items to be inherited by someone in particular, you can note that here, but remember that this is not legally binding, so all this does is indicate your intent to your family. It is far better to leave a legally binding list that reduces the risk of conflict. The list must be signed and dated and be specifically incorporated into your will. It is best to use an attorney who can ensure this is done properly.

In the meantime, this section will be a record of your important possessions and will ensure that the history and meaning behind these items will not be lost forever.

EXAMPLE

ITEM AND LOCATION	WHY IT IS IMPORTANT
Large red photo album in bookshelf	Contains photos, poetry, letters and diary written by George during First World War. Historical and sentimental value. To be kept in the family. More details are inside the front cover of the album.
Old papers in master bedroom drawer	Not to be thrown away. These are of historical value... may also be financially valuable. I want to leave these to Mary. More details are in the drawer.

ITEM AND LOCATION	WHY IT IS IMPORTANT

ITEM AND LOCATION	WHY IT IS IMPORTANT

ITEM AND LOCATION	WHY IT IS IMPORTANT

ITEM AND LOCATION	WHY IT IS IMPORTANT

ITEM AND LOCATION	WHY IT IS IMPORTANT

ITEM AND LOCATION	WHY IT IS IMPORTANT

ITEM AND LOCATION	WHY IT IS IMPORTANT

FINANCIAL

This section provides you with a concise summary of all the business contacts relating to your finances.

You may want to include such things as where you do your banking, where you have a bank safe deposit box and who has joint access, list brokerage or investment companies, online brokerage companies, where other stocks and bonds or other investments are held, certificates of deposit (noting maturity dates), life insurance policies, credit cards, store accounts, online accounts, frequent flier mile accounts, your accountant's contact information, the name of any attorney connected with any financial issues, mortgages, student loans, other loans, debts, etc.

If any account, investment, credit card, etc. is held jointly with another person, you might want to make note of this. Details of your sources of income will be noted in the next section (page 60).

Even though there is a space for it, I must recommend that you do not include account numbers, credit card numbers, reference numbers, PIN numbers or bank safe deposit box numbers in this organizer, just in case it falls into the wrong hands. You may prefer to keep a separate list of these numbers in a safe location. If you do choose to include any of this information, I urge you to keep this organizer in a safe place where it can be found only by you and those you trust.

EXAMPLE

SERVICE OR INVESTMENT	Bank Safe Deposit Box	NOTES
COMPANY AND CONTACT INFO	Savorspend Bank, Charlottesville Tel: XXX-XXX-XXXX	Cousin John (Tel: XXX-XXX-XXXX), has joint access ... has own key, and knows the number.
ACCOUNT #		
PAYMENT METHOD	Automatic deduction from checking account	
PAYMENT DUE DATE	Annually at year end	

SERVICE OR INVESTMENT	NOTES
COMPANY AND CONTACT INFO	
ACCOUNT #	
PAYMENT METHOD	
PAYMENT DUE DATE	

SERVICE OR INVESTMENT	NOTES
COMPANY AND CONTACT INFO	
ACCOUNT #	
PAYMENT METHOD	
PAYMENT DUE DATE	

SERVICE OR INVESTMENT	NOTES
COMPANY AND CONTACT INFO	
ACCOUNT #	
PAYMENT METHOD	
PAYMENT DUE DATE	

		NOTES
SERVICE OR INVESTMENT		
COMPANY AND CONTACT INFO		
ACCOUNT #		
PAYMENT METHOD		
PAYMENT DUE DATE		

		NOTES
SERVICE OR INVESTMENT		
COMPANY AND CONTACT INFO		
ACCOUNT #		
PAYMENT METHOD		
PAYMENT DUE DATE		

		NOTES
SERVICE OR INVESTMENT		
COMPANY AND CONTACT INFO		
ACCOUNT #		
PAYMENT METHOD		
PAYMENT DUE DATE		

SERVICE OR INVESTMENT		NOTES
COMPANY AND CONTACT INFO		
ACCOUNT #		
PAYMENT METHOD		
PAYMENT DUE DATE		

SERVICE OR INVESTMENT		NOTES
COMPANY AND CONTACT INFO		
ACCOUNT #		
PAYMENT METHOD		
PAYMENT DUE DATE		

SERVICE OR INVESTMENT		NOTES
COMPANY AND CONTACT INFO		
ACCOUNT #		
PAYMENT METHOD		
PAYMENT DUE DATE		

SERVICE OR INVESTMENT		NOTES
COMPANY AND CONTACT INFO		
ACCOUNT #		
PAYMENT METHOD		
PAYMENT DUE DATE		

SERVICE OR INVESTMENT		NOTES
COMPANY AND CONTACT INFO		
ACCOUNT #		
PAYMENT METHOD		
PAYMENT DUE DATE		

SERVICE OR INVESTMENT		NOTES
COMPANY AND CONTACT INFO		
ACCOUNT #		
PAYMENT METHOD		
PAYMENT DUE DATE		

SERVICE OR INVESTMENT		NOTES
COMPANY AND CONTACT INFO		
ACCOUNT #		
PAYMENT METHOD		
PAYMENT DUE DATE		

SERVICE OR INVESTMENT		NOTES
COMPANY AND CONTACT INFO		
ACCOUNT #		
PAYMENT METHOD		
PAYMENT DUE DATE		

SERVICE OR INVESTMENT		NOTES
COMPANY AND CONTACT INFO		
ACCOUNT #		
PAYMENT METHOD		
PAYMENT DUE DATE		

INCOME

This section should include all your regular sources of income, such as wages or salary from all employment, investment income, annuities, income from rental properties, Social Security, pensions, retirement income, government benefits, alimony, child support, etc.

Although there is a space allotted for account number, I must recommend that you be selective about what to include in this organizer, in case it falls into the wrong hands. This is especially the case for your Social Security number. You may prefer to keep a separate list of these numbers in a secure place. If you do choose to include this information, I recommend you keep this organizer in a safe place known only to you and those you trust.

EXAMPLE

TYPE OF INCOME	Salary	NOTES
SOURCE AND CONTACT INFO	University of Virginia Tel: XXX-XXX-XXXX	
ACCOUNT OR REFERENCE #	XXX XXX XXXXXXXXXXXXX	
PAYMENT METHOD	Direct deposit to checking account	
DATE RECEIVED	Last day of the month	

TYPE OF INCOME	NOTES
SOURCE AND CONTACT INFO	
ACCOUNT OR REFERENCE #	
PAYMENT METHOD	
DATE RECEIVED	

TYPE OF INCOME	NOTES
SOURCE AND CONTACT INFO	
ACCOUNT OR REFERENCE #	
PAYMENT METHOD	
DATE RECEIVED	

TYPE OF INCOME	NOTES
SOURCE AND CONTACT INFO	
ACCOUNT OR REFERENCE #	
PAYMENT METHOD	
DATE RECEIVED	

TYPE OF INCOME		NOTES
SOURCE AND CONTACT INFO		
ACCOUNT OR REFERENCE #		
PAYMENT METHOD		
DATE RECEIVED		

TYPE OF INCOME		NOTES
SOURCE AND CONTACT INFO		
ACCOUNT OR REFERENCE #		
PAYMENT METHOD		
DATE RECEIVED		

TYPE OF INCOME		NOTES
SOURCE AND CONTACT INFO		
ACCOUNT OR REFERENCE #		
PAYMENT METHOD		
DATE RECEIVED		

TYPE OF INCOME	NOTES
SOURCE AND CONTACT INFO	
ACCOUNT OR REFERENCE #	
PAYMENT METHOD	
DATE RECEIVED	

TYPE OF INCOME	NOTES
SOURCE AND CONTACT INFO	
ACCOUNT OR REFERENCE #	
PAYMENT METHOD	
DATE RECEIVED	

TYPE OF INCOME	NOTES
SOURCE AND CONTACT INFO	
ACCOUNT OR REFERENCE #	
PAYMENT METHOD	
DATE RECEIVED	

EMPLOYMENT

When you complete this section, think about whom you would want notified and what information would be needed if you were suddenly unable to work. If you are on salary, you may want to list your boss, a co-worker, professional license details, professional insurance details, etc.

If you're a business owner, you may wish to list contact information for a partner who could keep things going without you.

If you don't have a business partner, you may want to list more details, such as the name of your business; your work address and phone number; employees; client, customer, and vendor contact information; business licensing, insurance, property lease and contract details; alarm company; contact information for your accountants, bookkeepers, and attorneys; Internet connection, website and manager; advertising contacts; business property rental; the name of the bank where business funds or loans are held, and anything else that you consider important to note for your specific employment situation.

Professional subscriptions and memberships can either be listed here or on page 74.

EXAMPLE

BUSINESS CONNECTION	My boss	NOTES
COMPANY AND CONTACT INFO	Doolittle and Dallie Inc. Tel: XXX-XXX-XXXX	His secretary's name is Jane.
ACCOUNT OR REFERENCE #		

BUSINESS CONNECTION	Professional liability insurance	NOTES
COMPANY AND CONTACT INFO	Coversom Insurance Company Tel: XXX-XXX-XXXX	Premium is automatically deducted from my checking account annually on March 31.
ACCOUNT OR REFERENCE #	XXXXXXXXXXXXXXX	

BUSINESS CONNECTION	NOTES
COMPANY AND CONTACT INFO	
ACCOUNT OR REFERENCE #	

BUSINESS CONNECTION	NOTES
COMPANY AND CONTACT INFO	
ACCOUNT OR REFERENCE #	

BUSINESS CONNECTION	NOTES
COMPANY AND CONTACT INFO	
ACCOUNT OR REFERENCE #	

BUSINESS CONNECTION	NOTES
COMPANY AND CONTACT INFO	
ACCOUNT OR REFERENCE #	

BUSINESS CONNECTION	NOTES
COMPANY AND CONTACT INFO	
ACCOUNT OR REFERENCE #	

BUSINESS CONNECTION		NOTES
COMPANY AND CONTACT INFO		
ACCOUNT OR REFERENCE #		

BUSINESS CONNECTION		NOTES
COMPANY AND CONTACT INFO		
ACCOUNT OR REFERENCE #		

BUSINESS CONNECTION		NOTES
COMPANY AND CONTACT INFO		
ACCOUNT OR REFERENCE #		

BUSINESS CONNECTION		NOTES
COMPANY AND CONTACT INFO		
ACCOUNT OR REFERENCE #		

BUSINESS CONNECTION		NOTES
COMPANY AND CONTACT INFO		
ACCOUNT OR REFERENCE #		

BUSINESS CONNECTION	NOTES
COMPANY AND CONTACT INFO	
ACCOUNT OR REFERENCE #	

BUSINESS CONNECTION	NOTES
COMPANY AND CONTACT INFO	
ACCOUNT OR REFERENCE #	

BUSINESS CONNECTION	NOTES
COMPANY AND CONTACT INFO	
ACCOUNT OR REFERENCE #	

BUSINESS CONNECTION	NOTES
COMPANY AND CONTACT INFO	
ACCOUNT OR REFERENCE #	

BUSINESS CONNECTION	NOTES
COMPANY AND CONTACT INFO	
ACCOUNT OR REFERENCE #	

BUSINESS CONNECTION		NOTES
COMPANY AND CONTACT INFO		
ACCOUNT OR REFERENCE #		

BUSINESS CONNECTION		NOTES
COMPANY AND CONTACT INFO		
ACCOUNT OR REFERENCE #		

BUSINESS CONNECTION		NOTES
COMPANY AND CONTACT INFO		
ACCOUNT OR REFERENCE #		

BUSINESS CONNECTION		NOTES
COMPANY AND CONTACT INFO		
ACCOUNT OR REFERENCE #		

BUSINESS CONNECTION		NOTES
COMPANY AND CONTACT INFO		
ACCOUNT OR REFERENCE #		

BUSINESS CONNECTION	**NOTES**
COMPANY AND CONTACT INFO	
ACCOUNT OR REFERENCE #	

BUSINESS CONNECTION	**NOTES**
COMPANY AND CONTACT INFO	
ACCOUNT OR REFERENCE #	

BUSINESS CONNECTION	**NOTES**
COMPANY AND CONTACT INFO	
ACCOUNT OR REFERENCE #	

BUSINESS CONNECTION	**NOTES**
COMPANY AND CONTACT INFO	
ACCOUNT OR REFERENCE #	

BUSINESS CONNECTION	**NOTES**
COMPANY AND CONTACT INFO	
ACCOUNT OR REFERENCE #	

COMMITTEES AND BOARDS

In this section you should list all committees and boards with which you are involved. You may choose to list just one or two contact persons from each. Add any other relevant information that you think important to note.

EXAMPLE

COMMITTEE OR BOARD	Historic Home Restoration Committee	**NOTES**
CONTACT PERSON	Jo James (Chairperson)	I am a committee member.
PHONE NUMBER	XXX-XXX-XXXX	

COMMITTEE OR BOARD	Local School Board	**NOTES**
CONTACT PERSON	Jenny Jones (Chairperson)	I am a board member. Jenny's email is jenjonxyz@email.com.
PHONE NUMBER	XXX-XXX-XXXX	

COMMITTEE OR BOARD	Subdivision Home Owners Association	**NOTES**
CONTACT PERSON	Max Jones (Director)	I am treasurer.
PHONE NUMBER	XXX-XXX-XXXX	

COMMITTEE
OR BOARD

NOTES

CONTACT PERSON

PHONE NUMBER

COMMITTEE
OR BOARD

NOTES

CONTACT PERSON

PHONE NUMBER

COMMITTEE
OR BOARD

NOTES

CONTACT PERSON

PHONE NUMBER

COMMITTEE
OR BOARD

NOTES

CONTACT PERSON

PHONE NUMBER

COMMITTEE
OR BOARD

NOTES

CONTACT PERSON

PHONE NUMBER

COMMITTEE OR BOARD		NOTES
CONTACT PERSON		
PHONE NUMBER		

COMMITTEE OR BOARD		NOTES
CONTACT PERSON		
PHONE NUMBER		

COMMITTEE OR BOARD		NOTES
CONTACT PERSON		
PHONE NUMBER		

COMMITTEE OR BOARD		NOTES
CONTACT PERSON		
PHONE NUMBER		

COMMITTEE OR BOARD		NOTES
CONTACT PERSON		
PHONE NUMBER		

COMMITTEE OR BOARD	NOTES
CONTACT PERSON	
PHONE NUMBER	

COMMITTEE OR BOARD	NOTES
CONTACT PERSON	
PHONE NUMBER	

COMMITTEE OR BOARD	NOTES
CONTACT PERSON	
PHONE NUMBER	

COMMITTEE OR BOARD	NOTES
CONTACT PERSON	
PHONE NUMBER	

COMMITTEE OR BOARD	NOTES
CONTACT PERSON	
PHONE NUMBER	

SUBSCRIPTIONS AND MEMBERSHIPS

Subscriptions may be to newspapers, magazines, newsletters, etc. Don't forget to include online subscriptions.

Memberships may be to business or professional associations, trade unions, educational societies and associations, religious groups, interest clubs, gym memberships, sports teams, AARP, AAA, social clubs, etc.

EXAMPLE

SUBSCRIPTION OR MEMBERSHIP	Toneup Fitness Center membership	NOTES
CONTACT INFO	Tel: XXX-XXX-XXXX	
ACCOUNT #	XXXXXX	
PAYMENT METHOD	Automatic deduction from checking account	
PAYMENT DUE DATE	1st of month	

SUBSCRIPTION OR MEMBERSHIP	Professional Association membership	NOTES
CONTACT INFO	Tel: XXX-XXX-XXXX	
ACCOUNT #	XXXXXXX	
PAYMENT METHOD	VISA	
PAYMENT DUE DATE	Annually, March 31st	

SUBSCRIPTION OR MEMBERSHIP	NOTES
CONTACT INFO	
ACCOUNT #	
PAYMENT METHOD	
PAYMENT DUE DATE	

SUBSCRIPTION OR MEMBERSHIP	NOTES
CONTACT INFO	
ACCOUNT #	
PAYMENT METHOD	
PAYMENT DUE DATE	

SUBSCRIPTION OR MEMBERSHIP	NOTES
CONTACT INFO	
ACCOUNT #	
PAYMENT METHOD	
PAYMENT DUE DATE	

SUBSCRIPTION OR MEMBERSHIP		NOTES
CONTACT INFO		
ACCOUNT #		
PAYMENT METHOD		
PAYMENT DUE DATE		

SUBSCRIPTION OR MEMBERSHIP		NOTES
CONTACT INFO		
ACCOUNT #		
PAYMENT METHOD		
PAYMENT DUE DATE		

SUBSCRIPTION OR MEMBERSHIP		NOTES
CONTACT INFO		
ACCOUNT #		
PAYMENT METHOD		
PAYMENT DUE DATE		

SUBSCRIPTION OR MEMBERSHIP	NOTES
CONTACT INFO	
ACCOUNT #	
PAYMENT METHOD	
PAYMENT DUE DATE	

SUBSCRIPTION OR MEMBERSHIP	NOTES
CONTACT INFO	
ACCOUNT #	
PAYMENT METHOD	
PAYMENT DUE DATE	

SUBSCRIPTION OR MEMBERSHIP	NOTES
CONTACT INFO	
ACCOUNT #	
PAYMENT METHOD	
PAYMENT DUE DATE	

SUBSCRIPTION OR MEMBERSHIP		NOTES
CONTACT INFO		
ACCOUNT #		
PAYMENT METHOD		
PAYMENT DUE DATE		

SUBSCRIPTION OR MEMBERSHIP		NOTES
CONTACT INFO		
ACCOUNT #		
PAYMENT METHOD		
PAYMENT DUE DATE		

SUBSCRIPTION OR MEMBERSHIP		NOTES
CONTACT INFO		
ACCOUNT #		
PAYMENT METHOD		
PAYMENT DUE DATE		

SUBSCRIPTION OR MEMBERSHIP	NOTES
CONTACT INFO	
ACCOUNT #	
PAYMENT METHOD	
PAYMENT DUE DATE	

SUBSCRIPTION OR MEMBERSHIP	NOTES
CONTACT INFO	
ACCOUNT #	
PAYMENT METHOD	
PAYMENT DUE DATE	

SUBSCRIPTION OR MEMBERSHIP	NOTES
CONTACT INFO	
ACCOUNT #	
PAYMENT METHOD	
PAYMENT DUE DATE	

HEALTH INSURANCE

In this section you should note details about your primary health insurance, secondary insurance, long-term care insurance, dental plans, prescription plans, and give contact information for your health insurance agent, if you have one. If Medicare is one of your insurances, note which parts you have: part A (hospital insurance), part B (medical insurance), part C (Medicare Advantage, which usually covers all parts in one place with a Medicare-approved insurance plan), and/or part D (prescription drug coverage).

Some people pay their health insurance premium by check, but I do not recommend this because if you become ill or are injured, and do not pay your bill on time or within the "grace period," the insurance may be cancelled, just when you need it most. This can be avoided by arranging an automatic payment each month, either from your checking account or your credit card.

EXAMPLE

SERVICE	Primary health insurance	NOTES
COMPANY AND CONTACT INFO	Medicare Tel: XXX-XXX-XXXX	I have part A, part B, and part D.
ACCOUNT #	XXXXXXX	
PAYMENT METHOD	Automatic payments from credit card	
PAYMENT DUE DATE	Monthly on 2nd	

SERVICE	NOTES
COMPANY AND CONTACT INFO	
ACCOUNT #	
PAYMENT METHOD	
PAYMENT DUE DATE	

SERVICE	NOTES
COMPANY AND CONTACT INFO	
ACCOUNT #	
PAYMENT METHOD	
PAYMENT DUE DATE	

SERVICE	NOTES
COMPANY AND CONTACT INFO	
ACCOUNT #	
PAYMENT METHOD	
PAYMENT DUE DATE	

SERVICE		NOTES
COMPANY AND CONTACT INFO		
ACCOUNT #		
PAYMENT METHOD		
PAYMENT DUE DATE		

SERVICE		NOTES
COMPANY AND CONTACT INFO		
ACCOUNT #		
PAYMENT METHOD		
PAYMENT DUE DATE		

SERVICE		NOTES
COMPANY AND CONTACT INFO		
ACCOUNT #		
PAYMENT METHOD		
PAYMENT DUE DATE		

SERVICE

NOTES

COMPANY AND
CONTACT INFO

ACCOUNT #

PAYMENT METHOD

PAYMENT DUE DATE

SERVICE

NOTES

COMPANY AND
CONTACT INFO

ACCOUNT #

PAYMENT METHOD

PAYMENT DUE DATE

SERVICE

NOTES

COMPANY AND
CONTACT INFO

ACCOUNT #

PAYMENT METHOD

PAYMENT DUE DATE

MEDICAL INFORMATION

This section should help you record details of all of your present medical conditions and the doctors or facilities you go to for treatment.

Start with your primary care physician, and then your dentist, eye doctor, dermatologist, allergist, psychiatrist, counselor, chiropractor, acupuncturist, naturopath, physical therapist, other specialists, etc.

There is a space at the beginning for you to note your blood type. This could be important.

EXAMPLE

SERVICE	Primary Care Physician	NOTES
PROVIDER AND CONTACT INFO	Dr. Bernstein, Mytown Health Center Tel: XXX-XXX-XXX	
ACCOUNT #	XXXXXXX	
CONDITION	High blood pressure	
DATE OF ONSET	2013	
RESOLVED OR ONGOING	Ongoing	

BLOOD TYPE: ....

SERVICE	NOTES
PROVIDER AND CONTACT INFO	
ACCOUNT #	
CONDITION	
DATE OF ONSET	
RESOLVED OR ONGOING	

SERVICE	NOTES
PROVIDER AND CONTACT INFO	
ACCOUNT #	
CONDITION	
DATE OF ONSET	
RESOLVED OR ONGOING	

SERVICE		NOTES
PROVIDER AND CONTACT INFO		
ACCOUNT #		
CONDITION		
DATE OF ONSET		
RESOLVED OR ONGOING		

SERVICE		NOTES
PROVIDER AND CONTACT INFO		
ACCOUNT #		
CONDITION		
DATE OF ONSET		
RESOLVED OR ONGOING		

SERVICE		NOTES
PROVIDER AND CONTACT INFO		
ACCOUNT #		
CONDITION		
DATE OF ONSET		
RESOLVED OR ONGOING		

SERVICE		NOTES
PROVIDER AND CONTACT INFO		
ACCOUNT #		
CONDITION		
DATE OF ONSET		
RESOLVED OR ONGOING		

SERVICE		NOTES
PROVIDER AND CONTACT INFO		
ACCOUNT #		
CONDITION		
DATE OF ONSET		
RESOLVED OR ONGOING		

SERVICE		NOTES
PROVIDER AND CONTACT INFO		
ACCOUNT #		
CONDITION		
DATE OF ONSET		
RESOLVED OR ONGOING		

SERVICE		NOTES
PROVIDER AND CONTACT INFO		
ACCOUNT #		
CONDITION		
DATE OF ONSET		
RESOLVED OR ONGOING		

SERVICE		NOTES
PROVIDER AND CONTACT INFO		
ACCOUNT #		
CONDITION		
DATE OF ONSET		
RESOLVED OR ONGOING		

SERVICE		NOTES
PROVIDER AND CONTACT INFO		
ACCOUNT #		
CONDITION		
DATE OF ONSET		
RESOLVED OR ONGOING		

SERVICE		NOTES
PROVIDER AND CONTACT INFO		
ACCOUNT #		
CONDITION		
DATE OF ONSET		
RESOLVED OR ONGOING		

SERVICE	NOTES
PROVIDER AND CONTACT INFO	
ACCOUNT #	
CONDITION	
DATE OF ONSET	
RESOLVED OR ONGOING	

SERVICE	NOTES
PROVIDER AND CONTACT INFO	
ACCOUNT #	
CONDITION	
DATE OF ONSET	
RESOLVED OR ONGOING	

PRESCRIPTION MEDICATIONS

This section should list details of all of the medications prescribed for you, noting the reason for taking them, and the name of the prescribing doctor or specialist. If you no longer take a medication, try to give the date it was discontinued and the reason for discontinuing it (the condition may be cured, no longer an issue, or you may have a bad reaction to that particular medicine).

At the beginning you will find space in which you can make note of where and how you get your prescriptions filled.

It is a good idea to photocopy this information and leave one copy on your refrigerator and one copy in your purse or the glove compartment of your car. Rescue squads are trained to look in these places for information about you in an emergency situation.

Don't forget to update the information when prescriptions or other details change. This will be easier to do if you use pencil and an eraser, or pen and liquid paper.

EXAMPLE

MEDICATION	Expainex	NOTES, OR DATE DISCONTINUED (with reason)
PRESCRIBING DOCTOR	Dr. Bernstein (Primary Care Physician)	Discontinued in June 2013 because it made me feel nauseated
WHAT IT'S TAKEN FOR	Back pain	
DOSE AND HOW TAKEN	200mg, by mouth	
HOW OFTEN TAKEN	One in the morning and one at night	

WHERE PRESCRIPTIONS ARE FILLED:

PHARMACY 1 AND PHONE #: ....

PHARMACY 2 AND PHONE #: ....

MAIL ORDER/DELIVERY COMPANY: ....

PHONE NUMBER OR WEBSITE: ....

	NOTES, OR DATE DISCONTINUED (with reason)
MEDICATION	
PRESCRIBING DOCTOR	
WHAT IT'S TAKEN FOR	
DOSE AND HOW TAKEN	
HOW OFTEN TAKEN	

	NOTES, OR DATE DISCONTINUED (with reason)
MEDICATION	
PRESCRIBING DOCTOR	
WHAT IT'S TAKEN FOR	
DOSE AND HOW TAKEN	
HOW OFTEN TAKEN	

MEDICATION		NOTES, OR DATE DISCONTINUED (with reason)
PRESCRIBING DOCTOR		
WHAT IT'S TAKEN FOR		
DOSE AND HOW TAKEN		
HOW OFTEN TAKEN		

MEDICATION		NOTES, OR DATE DISCONTINUED (with reason)
PRESCRIBING DOCTOR		
WHAT IT'S TAKEN FOR		
DOSE AND HOW TAKEN		
HOW OFTEN TAKEN		

MEDICATION		NOTES, OR DATE DISCONTINUED (with reason)
PRESCRIBING DOCTOR		
WHAT IT'S TAKEN FOR		
DOSE AND HOW TAKEN		
HOW OFTEN TAKEN		

MEDICATION	NOTES, OR DATE DISCONTINUED (with reason)
PRESCRIBING DOCTOR	
WHAT IT'S TAKEN FOR	
DOSE AND HOW TAKEN	
HOW OFTEN TAKEN	

MEDICATION	NOTES, OR DATE DISCONTINUED (with reason)
PRESCRIBING DOCTOR	
WHAT IT'S TAKEN FOR	
DOSE AND HOW TAKEN	
HOW OFTEN TAKEN	

MEDICATION	NOTES, OR DATE DISCONTINUED (with reason)
PRESCRIBING DOCTOR	
WHAT IT'S TAKEN FOR	
DOSE AND HOW TAKEN	
HOW OFTEN TAKEN	

MEDICATION		NOTES, OR DATE DISCONTINUED (with reason)
PRESCRIBING DOCTOR		
WHAT IT'S TAKEN FOR		
DOSE AND HOW TAKEN		
HOW OFTEN TAKEN		

MEDICATION		NOTES, OR DATE DISCONTINUED (with reason)
PRESCRIBING DOCTOR		
WHAT IT'S TAKEN FOR		
DOSE AND HOW TAKEN		
HOW OFTEN TAKEN		

MEDICATION		NOTES, OR DATE DISCONTINUED (with reason)
PRESCRIBING DOCTOR		
WHAT IT'S TAKEN FOR		
DOSE AND HOW TAKEN		
HOW OFTEN TAKEN		

MEDICATION	NOTES, OR DATE DISCONTINUED (with reason)
PRESCRIBING DOCTOR	
WHAT IT'S TAKEN FOR	
DOSE AND HOW TAKEN	
HOW OFTEN TAKEN	

MEDICATION	NOTES, OR DATE DISCONTINUED (with reason)
PRESCRIBING DOCTOR	
WHAT IT'S TAKEN FOR	
DOSE AND HOW TAKEN	
HOW OFTEN TAKEN	

MEDICATION	NOTES, OR DATE DISCONTINUED (with reason)
PRESCRIBING DOCTOR	
WHAT IT'S TAKEN FOR	
DOSE AND HOW TAKEN	
HOW OFTEN TAKEN	

MEDICATION		NOTES, OR DATE DISCONTINUED (with reason)
PRESCRIBING DOCTOR		
WHAT IT'S TAKEN FOR		
DOSE AND HOW TAKEN		
HOW OFTEN TAKEN		

MEDICATION		NOTES, OR DATE DISCONTINUED (with reason)
PRESCRIBING DOCTOR		
WHAT IT'S TAKEN FOR		
DOSE AND HOW TAKEN		
HOW OFTEN TAKEN		

MEDICATION		NOTES, OR DATE DISCONTINUED (with reason)
PRESCRIBING DOCTOR		
WHAT IT'S TAKEN FOR		
DOSE AND HOW TAKEN		
HOW OFTEN TAKEN		

MEDICATION	NOTES, OR DATE DISCONTINUED (with reason)
PRESCRIBING DOCTOR	
WHAT IT'S TAKEN FOR	
DOSE AND HOW TAKEN	
HOW OFTEN TAKEN	

MEDICATION	NOTES, OR DATE DISCONTINUED (with reason)
PRESCRIBING DOCTOR	
WHAT IT'S TAKEN FOR	
DOSE AND HOW TAKEN	
HOW OFTEN TAKEN	

MEDICATION	NOTES, OR DATE DISCONTINUED (with reason)
PRESCRIBING DOCTOR	
WHAT IT'S TAKEN FOR	
DOSE AND HOW TAKEN	
HOW OFTEN TAKEN	

VITAMINS AND SUPPLEMENTS

In this section you should list all over-the-counter vitamins and supplements you take and should say how and why you take them.

Don't forget to update this information when details change. This will be easier to do if you use pencil and an eraser, or pen and liquid paper.

EXAMPLE

This is not intended as medical advice. If you need vitamins and supplements you should seek the advice of a medical professional.

		NOTES, OR DATE DISCONTINUED (with reason)
WHAT I TAKE	Vitamin D	
WHAT IT'S TAKEN FOR	To aid calcium absorption	
DOSE AND HOW TAKEN	1500 IU, by mouth	
HOW OFTEN TAKEN	Each morning	

		NOTES, OR DATE DISCONTINUED (with reason)
WHAT I TAKE	Flaxseed oil	
WHAT IT'S TAKEN FOR	To help maintain good blood cholesterol levels	
DOSE AND HOW TAKEN	1000 mg, by mouth	
HOW OFTEN TAKEN	Twice daily	

WHAT I TAKE

NOTES, OR DATE DISCONTINUED
(with reason)

WHAT IT'S
TAKEN FOR

DOSE AND
HOW TAKEN

HOW OFTEN TAKEN

WHAT I TAKE

NOTES, OR DATE DISCONTINUED
(with reason)

WHAT IT'S
TAKEN FOR

DOSE AND
HOW TAKEN

HOW OFTEN TAKEN

WHAT I TAKE

NOTES, OR DATE DISCONTINUED
(with reason)

WHAT IT'S
TAKEN FOR

DOSE AND
HOW TAKEN

HOW OFTEN TAKEN

WHAT I TAKE

NOTES, OR DATE DISCONTINUED
(with reason)

WHAT IT'S
TAKEN FOR

DOSE AND
HOW TAKEN

HOW OFTEN TAKEN

WHAT I TAKE		NOTES, OR DATE DISCONTINUED (with reason)
WHAT IT'S TAKEN FOR		
DOSE AND HOW TAKEN		
HOW OFTEN TAKEN		

WHAT I TAKE		NOTES, OR DATE DISCONTINUED (with reason)
WHAT IT'S TAKEN FOR		
DOSE AND HOW TAKEN		
HOW OFTEN TAKEN		

WHAT I TAKE		NOTES, OR DATE DISCONTINUED (with reason)
WHAT IT'S TAKEN FOR		
DOSE AND HOW TAKEN		
HOW OFTEN TAKEN		

WHAT I TAKE		NOTES, OR DATE DISCONTINUED (with reason)
WHAT IT'S TAKEN FOR		
DOSE AND HOW TAKEN		
HOW OFTEN TAKEN		

WHAT I TAKE		NOTES, OR DATE DISCONTINUED (with reason)
WHAT IT'S TAKEN FOR		
DOSE AND HOW TAKEN		
HOW OFTEN TAKEN		

WHAT I TAKE		NOTES, OR DATE DISCONTINUED (with reason)
WHAT IT'S TAKEN FOR		
DOSE AND HOW TAKEN		
HOW OFTEN TAKEN		

WHAT I TAKE		NOTES, OR DATE DISCONTINUED (with reason)
WHAT IT'S TAKEN FOR		
DOSE AND HOW TAKEN		
HOW OFTEN TAKEN		

WHAT I TAKE		NOTES, OR DATE DISCONTINUED (with reason)
WHAT IT'S TAKEN FOR		
DOSE AND HOW TAKEN		
HOW OFTEN TAKEN		

WHAT I TAKE		NOTES, OR DATE DISCONTINUED (with reason)
WHAT IT'S TAKEN FOR		
DOSE AND HOW TAKEN		
HOW OFTEN TAKEN		

WHAT I TAKE		NOTES, OR DATE DISCONTINUED (with reason)
WHAT IT'S TAKEN FOR		
DOSE AND HOW TAKEN		
HOW OFTEN TAKEN		

WHAT I TAKE		NOTES, OR DATE DISCONTINUED (with reason)
WHAT IT'S TAKEN FOR		
DOSE AND HOW TAKEN		
HOW OFTEN TAKEN		

WHAT I TAKE		NOTES, OR DATE DISCONTINUED (with reason)
WHAT IT'S TAKEN FOR		
DOSE AND HOW TAKEN		
HOW OFTEN TAKEN		

WHAT I TAKE	**NOTES, OR DATE DISCONTINUED** (with reason)
WHAT IT'S TAKEN FOR	
DOSE AND HOW TAKEN	
HOW OFTEN TAKEN	

WHAT I TAKE	**NOTES, OR DATE DISCONTINUED** (with reason)
WHAT IT'S TAKEN FOR	
DOSE AND HOW TAKEN	
HOW OFTEN TAKEN	

WHAT I TAKE	**NOTES, OR DATE DISCONTINUED** (with reason)
WHAT IT'S TAKEN FOR	
DOSE AND HOW TAKEN	
HOW OFTEN TAKEN	

WHAT I TAKE	**NOTES, OR DATE DISCONTINUED** (with reason)
WHAT IT'S TAKEN FOR	
DOSE AND HOW TAKEN	
HOW OFTEN TAKEN	

ALLERGIES AND BAD REACTIONS

This section should record everything that causes you to have an allergic or bad reaction. This information could help those around you ensure that you are not given something you should not have, which could be essential in a situation where you are unable to communicate.

Remember to list allergies or bad reactions to medicines, foods, lotions, perfumes, and environmental triggers. Make a note of everything that might help someone assist you in an emergency situation.

EXAMPLE

This is not intended as medical advice. If you have allergies or bad reactions, always seek the advice of a medical professional.

WHAT I AM ALLERGIC TO	Shrimp	NOTES
ACTION TO TAKE IF I HAVE A BAD REACTION	Use my EpiPen (always in my purse), and get me to the emergency room.	I have a serious reaction and may not be able to breathe. The EpiPen works!

WHAT I AM ALLERGIC TO	Penicillin	NOTES
ACTION TO TAKE IF I HAVE A BAD REACTION	Take me to the emergency room.	I can have trouble breathing.

WHAT I AM ALLERGIC TO		NOTES
ACTION TO TAKE IF I HAVE A BAD REACTION		

WHAT I AM ALLERGIC TO		NOTES
ACTION TO TAKE IF I HAVE A BAD REACTION		

WHAT I AM ALLERGIC TO		NOTES
ACTION TO TAKE IF I HAVE A BAD REACTION		

WHAT I AM ALLERGIC TO		NOTES
ACTION TO TAKE IF I HAVE A BAD REACTION		

WHAT I AM ALLERGIC TO		NOTES
ACTION TO TAKE IF I HAVE A BAD REACTION		

WHAT I AM ALLERGIC TO		NOTES
ACTION TO TAKE IF I HAVE A BAD REACTION		

WHAT I AM ALLERGIC TO		NOTES
ACTION TO TAKE IF I HAVE A BAD REACTION		

WHAT I AM ALLERGIC TO		NOTES
ACTION TO TAKE IF I HAVE A BAD REACTION		

WHAT I AM ALLERGIC TO		NOTES
ACTION TO TAKE IF I HAVE A BAD REACTION		

WHAT I AM ALLERGIC TO		NOTES
ACTION TO TAKE IF I HAVE A BAD REACTION		

WHAT I AM ALLERGIC TO		NOTES
ACTION TO TAKE IF I HAVE A BAD REACTION		

WHAT I AM ALLERGIC TO		NOTES
ACTION TO TAKE IF I HAVE A BAD REACTION		

SURGICAL HISTORY

Record all operations you have had, with the approximate date they were performed. Note the condition that made the operation necessary and the status of that condition now.

EXAMPLE

SURGERY	Knee replacement	NOTES
DATE	2013	
REASON	Arthritis	
OUTCOME	Recovered	

SURGERY	Gall bladder removal	NOTES
DATE	2008	
REASON	Gallstones	
OUTCOME	Recovered	

		NOTES
SURGERY		
DATE		
REASON		
OUTCOME		

		NOTES
SURGERY		
DATE		
REASON		
OUTCOME		

		NOTES
SURGERY		
DATE		
REASON		
OUTCOME		

SURGERY		NOTES
DATE		
REASON		
OUTCOME		

SURGERY		NOTES
DATE		
REASON		
OUTCOME		

SURGERY		NOTES
DATE		
REASON		
OUTCOME		

SURGERY		NOTES
DATE		
REASON		
OUTCOME		

SURGERY		NOTES
DATE		
REASON		
OUTCOME		

SURGERY		NOTES
DATE		
REASON		
OUTCOME		

FAMILY MEDICAL HISTORY

Over time we lose details of our family history, so making this record will not only be of use to you, but may also give invaluable information to younger family members in the future.

Some conditions run in families, so when you complete this section, be sure not to forget any of the following inheritable diseases:

Cardiovascular disease	Anxiety
Heart problems	Depression
Breast cancer	Psychiatric illness
Colon cancer	Severe memory loss
Prostate cancer	Severe arthritis

LIST BELOW ANY DISEASES THAT RUN IN YOUR FAMILY

_____

_____

_____

_____

_____

_____

_____

_____

RELATIVE		NOTES
BIRTH DATE		
MEDICAL CONDITIONS		
DATE OR AGE DECEASED		
CAUSE OF DEATH		

RELATIVE		NOTES
BIRTH DATE		
MEDICAL CONDITIONS		
DATE OR AGE DECEASED		
CAUSE OF DEATH		

RELATIVE		NOTES
BIRTH DATE		
MEDICAL CONDITIONS		
DATE OR AGE DECEASED		
CAUSE OF DEATH		

RELATIVE		NOTES
BIRTH DATE		
MEDICAL CONDITIONS		
DATE OR AGE DECEASED		
CAUSE OF DEATH		

RELATIVE		NOTES
BIRTH DATE		
MEDICAL CONDITIONS		
DATE OR AGE DECEASED		
CAUSE OF DEATH		

RELATIVE		NOTES
BIRTH DATE		
MEDICAL CONDITIONS		
DATE OR AGE DECEASED		
CAUSE OF DEATH		

RELATIVE	NOTES
BIRTH DATE	
MEDICAL CONDITIONS	
DATE OR AGE DECEASED	
CAUSE OF DEATH	

RELATIVE	NOTES
BIRTH DATE	
MEDICAL CONDITIONS	
DATE OR AGE DECEASED	
CAUSE OF DEATH	

RELATIVE	NOTES
BIRTH DATE	
MEDICAL CONDITIONS	
DATE OR AGE DECEASED	
CAUSE OF DEATH	

ESTATE PLANNING RECORDS

This section lets your loved ones know what documents you have, as well as who is named for positions of responsibility and how to contact them. Please refer to page 5 for more information about estate planning and the documents you need.

You may want to include your information for the following:

- A will and/or trust

- Durable general power of attorney

- Medical power of attorney

- Advance medical directive

- A record of your prepaid funeral plan or a note of your wishes—if you don't already have this, the section beginning on page 130 will guide you

- Any other documents you feel are relevant to your situation.

EXAMPLE

DOCUMENT	Will	NOTES
RESPONSIBILITY	Executor	Mary (daughter) is listed second, Tel: XXX-XXX-XXX. She has a copy of my will at her house.
PERSON NAMED AND CONTACT INFO	Joe, my husband XXX-XXX-XXXX (mobile)	

DOCUMENT	Funeral wishes	NOTES
RESPONSIBILITY		This is written into my will, but there are more details on page 130.
PERSON NAMED AND CONTACT INFO		

DOCUMENT	NOTES
RESPONSIBILITY	
PERSON NAMED AND CONTACT INFO	

DOCUMENT	NOTES
RESPONSIBILITY	
PERSON NAMED AND CONTACT INFO	

DOCUMENT	NOTES
RESPONSIBILITY	
PERSON NAMED AND CONTACT INFO	

DOCUMENT	NOTES
RESPONSIBILITY	
PERSON NAMED AND CONTACT INFO	

DOCUMENT	NOTES
RESPONSIBILITY	
PERSON NAMED AND CONTACT INFO	

DOCUMENT		NOTES
RESPONSIBILITY		
PERSON NAMED AND CONTACT INFO		

DOCUMENT		NOTES
RESPONSIBILITY		
PERSON NAMED AND CONTACT INFO		

DOCUMENT		NOTES
RESPONSIBILITY		
PERSON NAMED AND CONTACT INFO		

DOCUMENT		NOTES
RESPONSIBILITY		
PERSON NAMED AND CONTACT INFO		

DOCUMENT		NOTES
RESPONSIBILITY		
PERSON NAMED AND CONTACT INFO		

DOCUMENT	NOTES
RESPONSIBILITY	
PERSON NAMED AND CONTACT INFO	

DOCUMENT	NOTES
RESPONSIBILITY	
PERSON NAMED AND CONTACT INFO	

DOCUMENT	NOTES
RESPONSIBILITY	
PERSON NAMED AND CONTACT INFO	

DOCUMENT	NOTES
RESPONSIBILITY	
PERSON NAMED AND CONTACT INFO	

DOCUMENT	NOTES
RESPONSIBILITY	
PERSON NAMED AND CONTACT INFO	

UNOFFICIAL ADVANCE
MEDICAL DIRECTIVE

An advance medical directive lets doctors and family know how you want to be treated if you are in the hospital and close to death with no chance of meaningful recovery.

If you have advance medical directive documents and have recorded where they can be found on page 135, you can ignore this section.

However, if you don't have documents you may want to consider making note of your wishes here, until you can get legal documents drawn up. COMPLETING THIS SECTION DOES NOT MAKE IT A LEGAL DOCUMENT, NOR DOES IT REPLACE THE NEED FOR ONE, but leaving these unofficial instructions is better than leaving no guidance at all.

The reason for leaving these instructions is so that you don't put your loved ones in the difficult situation of having to decide what kind of treatment you will get. The worst scenario is when family members cannot agree on what to do—this is potentially a highly charged situation that can cause enormous rifts or feelings of guilt or anger.

In addition, if you know that you would not wish to be resuscitated if you had a life-threatening event such as a heart attack, you can leave a "do-not-resuscitate" order with your doctor or hospital. They will help you to complete the necessary forms.

MY UNOFFICIAL ADVANCE MEDICAL DIRECTIVE

(A note of my wishes until I can get legal documents drawn up)

THE OPTIONS	CHECK ONE	EXTRA NOTES/COMMENTS FOR LOVED ONES
If I am unable to communicate and the doctor tells you that I am dying or that my condition is so bad that I will never be aware of myself or of my surroundings again, please take me off machines or treatments that are keeping me alive artificially. Just keep me comfortable and out of pain and allow me to die naturally.		
If I am unable to communicate and the doctor tells you that I am dying or that my condition is so bad that I will never be aware of myself or of my surroundings again, keep me on all machines and treatments that will keep my body alive as long as possible. Only when the doctor tells you that the limit of generally accepted health care standards has been reached should this treatment be stopped.		
Please make the decision for me based upon the advice the doctor gives you. *List who should make this decision. It may be best to choose one person to eliminate the possibility of disagreement, or an odd number of people—so that if they disagree, a majority decision can be reached.*		Who should make this decision:

Sign and date:

UNOFFICIAL ORGAN DONATION DIRECTIVE

If you have a will properly drawn up by an attorney, it should already include instructions about organ donation. You should also note your wishes on your driver's license, but do ensure that both documents say the same thing, and let your family members know your decision. If you have done this, you will not need to complete this section, but if you do, it will serve as an unofficial record of your wishes.

The rules in each state differ throughout the US, but an attorney can make sure your documentation is correct for your particular area. For example, currently in Virginia, if you have left organ donation instructions either through an advance medical directive or on your driver's license, the physicians must honor your instructions. If you have not left such instructions, there is a presumption that they may take your organs, though the family members are entitled to object to this.

COMPLETING THIS SECTION DOES NOT MAKE IT A LEGAL DOCUMENT, NOR DOES IT REPLACE THE NEED FOR ONE, but leaving these unofficial instructions (until you can have proper documents drawn up) and discussing it with your family or friends is better than leaving no indication of your wishes at all.

MY UNOFFICIAL ORGAN DONATION DIRECTIVE

(A note of my wishes until I can get legal documents drawn up)

THE OPTIONS	CHECK ONE OR MORE	SIGN AND DATE
I want my medical power of attorney to decide for me.		
I do not want to be an organ donor.		
I want to donate any organs needed.		
I want to donate just tissue, like skin or bone.		
I want to donate corneas from my eyes.		
I want to donate my body for research or educational programs.		
OTHER INSTRUCTIONS:		

OBITUARY GUIDE

If you have already written a note of details that could be included in your obituary, you can ignore this section and simply say where these notes can be found by using the document locator chart at the back of this organizer.

Some people prefer not to think about their obituary and leave it for family or friends to decide what to write when the time comes. However, the person who knows best what should be included is you, so you may want to make a few notes now and make it easier for your family and friends when the time comes.

The following pages are intended to be a guide to help you think of details to include. Not everything will apply to you, so you might leave some spaces empty, or alter and adapt them to make them yours. Write in as much detail as you can.

If something happens to you, this information will be needed quickly, so I recommend letting your trusted family and friends know that these details are included in this organizer.

EXAMPLE

DETAIL	NOTES
Educational facilities I attended	Southall High School, Worcester, then Northall College, then after working a few years, attended Huyton College for Occupational Therapy.
My spouse	John Ray, dearly loved but he died in 1980. I am now with my partner John Doe ... also dearly loved.

DETAIL	NOTES
Where and when I was born	
My mother and father	
My brothers and sisters	
My spouse or partner	
My children	

DETAIL	NOTES
My grandchildren	
My great-grandchildren	
Important friends	
Schools, colleges and scholastic achievements	
Personal experiences or achievements	

DETAIL	NOTES
Professional experiences or achievements	
Special interests or volunteering	
Other important details or events	

FUNERAL OR CREMATION WISHES

Although this is not something we want to think about, if we make a note of our funeral or memorial wishes now, well before we need to, we relieve our loved ones of the stress of having to make these decisions for us.

The following chart should help you organize your thoughts. Not everything will apply to you, so just fill in the spaces you want and add information to make it your own.

Some people will already have made arrangements for their funeral and burial, and may have paid for it in advance. If this is the case, make sure that your family or friends know, and make a note of it here, giving contact details of the company to whom you have given your instructions, and note where your copy of the contract can be found.

If something happens to you, this information will be needed quickly, so I recommend discussing your wishes with your family members and letting your trusted family and friends know that details are written in this organizer.

EXAMPLE

DETAIL	NOTES
What kind of ceremony it should be	*I want a traditional service and burial.*
Where the ceremony should take place	*St. Mary's Church, Whitton*

DETAIL	NOTES
Prepaid funeral plan	Company contact info: Where my copy of the contract can be found:

Or if you don't have a prepaid funeral plan:

What kind of ceremony it should be	
Where the ceremony should take place	
Who should lead the ceremony	
Music choice	

DETAIL	NOTES
Words to be spoken	
Readings	
Coffin type	
Burial place	
Headstone	
Where cremation should take place	

DETAIL	NOTES
What should be done with the ashes	

DOCUMENT LOCATOR CHART

Documents won't help you at all—unless you (or the right person) can find them when they need to be found. The following charts allow you to record where your documents are located. You may want to refer to page 8 if you are not sure where to keep them.

If you keep documents in a secure place at home, ensure that only your trusted family and friends know where this place is. If you have a bank safe deposit box, make sure you record details of this in the Financial section of this organizer. Protect your Social Security number and Employer ID number by keeping them in a safe place, where the wrong person cannot find them.

Use the blank spaces to record the location of any other documents not listed that you feel are imporant to you. Business owners should include the location of their critical business documents.

If you have lost any of your important documents, I suggest asking your attorney or looking online to find out how you can get them replaced.

EXAMPLE

DOCUMENT	BANK SAFE DEPOSIT BOX	SECURE PLACE AT HOME	WITH ATTORNEY	OTHER PLACES
Will or trust		Copy	✓	
Social Security number	✓	✓		My tax preparer also has this number in her records.

Make notes of where your originals and copies can be found.

DOCUMENT	BANK SAFE DEPOSIT BOX	SECURE PLACE AT HOME	WITH ATTORNEY	OTHER PLACES
Will				
Trust				
Durable general power of attorney documents				
Medical power of attorney documents				
Advance medical directive				

Make notes of where your originals and copies can be found.

DOCUMENT	BANK SAFE DEPOSIT BOX	SECURE PLACE AT HOME	WITH ATTORNEY	OTHER PLACES
Prepaid funeral plan documents				
Social Security number (remember this should not be accessible to the wrong person)				
Birth certificate				
Naturalization certificate				
Passport				

Make notes of where your originals and copies can be found.

DOCUMENT	BANK SAFE DEPOSIT BOX	SECURE PLACE AT HOME	WITH ATTORNEY	OTHER PLACES
Marriage certificate				
Adoption papers				
Divorce decree				
Military service documents				
List of finance account numbers or reference numbers (if not included already—see page 54)				

Make notes of where your originals and copies can be found.

DOCUMENT	BANK SAFE DEPOSIT BOX	SECURE PLACE AT HOME	WITH ATTORNEY	OTHER PLACES
Financial certificates				
Copies of state and federal tax returns				
Health insurance and/or Medicare cards				
Insurance policies				
Appraisals for household valuables, antiques or jewelry				

Make notes of where your originals and copies can be found.

DOCUMENT	BANK SAFE DEPOSIT BOX	SECURE PLACE AT HOME	WITH ATTORNEY	OTHER PLACES
Property deeds				
Mortgage agreements				
Loan agreements				
Vehicle titles				
Other legal agreements				

Make notes of where your originals and copies can be found.

DOCUMENT	BANK SAFE DEPOSIT BOX	SECURE PLACE AT HOME	WITH ATTORNEY	OTHER PLACES
Educational certificates				
Professional certificates or licenses				
List of computer passwords				

Make notes of where your originals and copies can be found.

DOCUMENT	BANK SAFE DEPOSIT BOX	SECURE PLACE AT HOME	WITH ATTORNEY	OTHER PLACES

{WHAT'S NEXT?}

One step further

When completed, this organizer should provide you with a thorough and detailed record of your life, which will enable you to stay in control of your personal affairs. However, it also serves as a guide for your loved ones, should you need their assistance, and it relieves them of the burden of gathering this information in an emergency situation or upon your death.

Because of this, it is important to let those you trust know that you have this organizer and where to find it, and be sure that your executors will be able to access it when the need arises.

It will have taken time and trouble to complete this task, but by carrying it out not only are you enabling your own life to run smoothly, you will also be passing on the gifts of clarity and peace of mind to those dearest to you, and on whom you may one day come to rely. Take time to keep it updated as the years pass, for you never know what lies ahead.

I urge you to encourage your family and friends also to complete an organizer so they too may benefit from having their own *Records to the Rescue!*

Christine Ballard

NOTES

NOTES

NOTES

NOTES

NOTES

NOTES

NOTES

NOTES

Made in the USA
Middletown, DE
01 October 2021

49470229R00091